A One Winged Angel

André de Korvin

TRANSCENDENT ZERO PRESS
HOUSTON, TEXAS

PUBLISHED BY TRANSCENDENT ZERO PRESS
www.transcendentzeropress.org

ISBN-13: 978-1-946460-07-3
Library of Congress Control Number: 2020931468

Printed in the United States of America

Transcendent Zero Press
16429 El Camino Real Apt. #7
Houston, TX 77062

Cover painting: "Classic Notes" by Evelyn Roper
Cover design: Glynn Monroe Irby

FIRST EDITION

A One Winged Angel

André de Korvin

Dedicated To My Wonderful Wife Yi Lin

TABLE OF CONTENTS

A One Winged Angel
Introduction

by Gail Tirone

Among the many fine poets I have known, André de Korvin stands out. His images are startling. Original. These poems are powerful – a tour-de-force. There's just so much there. De Korvin's complex world view entices the reader to join him on a dream journey. His narrator, part voyager, part voyeur, circumnavigates a world whose most fundamental elements, from time to weather, are subject to violence and imbued with profound emotions.

> A wounded sky stumbles
> and falls bruised and
> bloodied by the evening sun.

In de Korvin's poems, time melds into weather and is anthropomorphized almost beyond recognition.

> People in the rain passing by
> like deported tomorrows
> and the future turning to stare
> at you with its pale eyes.

As you grow immersed in this book, you begin to grasp the grammar of de Korvin's world, where clocks, train stations, violins, the color blue and other paraphernalia of ordinary life become signposts on an extraordinary journey. De Korvin invites you to join him on

> …a narrow road circling
> a gas station at the edge of the sky
> …[where] newspapers unfolding their wings
> …rise over the rooftops of the world.

The writer and his conscientiousness are ever-present in this volume, and the poems give voice to where poems are and how poems happen: "a poem loiters in a deserted parking lot," "his breath deposits poems on the pale ceiling of the room" and even "we would inadvertently inhale poems like smoke my father inhaled from his Gauloise Bleue."

The poet's relationship with the poem is one of yearning.

> Sipping coffee, I look
> through my many windows
> and wait for a poem
> to drive by.

The urge to write is a visceral craving.

> I lie in my star-shaped bed,
> jab a rusted pen
> deep into my bruised veins.
> Ink flows inside my body.

The poetic process is an alchemy of heightened awareness, struggle and chance, and in de Korvin's case, one where keen observations run through a fertile imagination, turn to gold. Of those unfortunates who don't read poetry, de Korvin declares:

> Many… never knowing they were grieving
> poetry, unread stanzas a darkness
> on the pale halos of their gods.

The insights of these poems, while intensely personal, are also universal. The son of Russian immigrants, de Korvin was raised in Paris, attended university in California and has spent much of his adult life in Texas. Growing up in Paris among White Russian exiles, de Korvin is intimately familiar with the sense of displacement. The poet in these poems is lost, a *flaneur* perambulating the city of Paris, searching for bridges that no longer exist, under chestnut trees and the heavy Paris sky. Paris is a touchstone in the poems – a wormhole in time through which the reader falls, traveling decades in a single stanza.

Train stations punctuate the poems, more emblems of search than arrival. *La Gare St. Lazare*, one of Paris' largest stations, is mentioned repeatedly – the station where time runs backwards. As the poet-as-a-young-man wanders through the station, he runs again and again through *La Salle des Pas Perdus*, literally the Hall of the lost foorsteps or more mundanely rendered as Waiting Room. *La Gare St. Lazare* becomes a murmuring, hypnotic incantation, a talisman, a portent of loss and suspended time.

When you were ten, you killed time
walking the halls of La Gare St. Lazare,
running back and forth
through La Salle des Pas Perdus,
feeling lost amid the station's clocks,
their hands pointing to void spaces in-between hours.
Today, tricking your mind, clocks run counter
clock wise, their revolution erasing our moments.

One of the most extraordinary poems in the collection, "Running to Dark Waters and White Clouds," traverses time and geography like hopscotch, from winding Paris alleys to California dreaming to Houston's Buffalo Bayou. The narrative pivots, moment to moment, from German bombs to Texas floods and college textbooks of "math fuzzy as metaphysics." Time shifts into reverse, and the poem concludes with a moving crescendo of pre-birth memories: de Korvin's poetic virtuoso is evident as he defines the experience in terms that are at once astoundingly original yet oddly familiar.

In between contractions your mother dreams
dark waters and white clouds.
Nazis parade in Berlin.

You are vapor rising in your mother's dream.
You sense the depth of currents, the presence of iron,
electric pulses running through your world,
the transparent film wrapped around your body,
the thin cord that ties you to this planet, you hear
distant echoes of French and Russian conversations.
Over dark waters, below white clouds
you are pure potential, pure possibility.

…Before, you slept in no space, no time.
Your mother's heartbeats were
songs sung softly just for you.

De Korvin explores the metaphysics of the disenfranchised – stateless immigrants, refugees, the homeless, the unemployed and the unlucky. In his lexicon, the homeless are "cardboard angels," and he decries the plight of homelessness and condemns the world's seeming indifference.

> Days stumble, a procession of homeless
> …I stare at the sky and sometimes the sky
> blushes, guilt written all over it.

In "The Best," de Korvin disputes that the best things in life – like sunsets – are free. His empathy is palpable, and the image stays with you like a slap felt long after the hand is gone.

> No sunset for the starving
> only a broken egg dripping
> on the blue cloth of the sky.

The dark notes in this volume reflect our dark times. And yet moments of hope and redemption flicker through the poems. In "The University" the underdogs imagine overcoming adversity: "Free at last we'll hail fast moving clouds with star-shaped hands." In another poem, burdens are lifted and you are:

> …suddenly lighter than
> one third of a humming bird song
> so your laughter unzips the sky
> and you can only
> remember the sun…

In "Long Sleep Motel," an homage to Baudelaire, de Korvin ponders "the language of flowers and mute things."
He articulates the pathos of art and beauty arrested, when the wind speaks and says, "*a violin sleeps in the aching heart of every rose.*"
True, the violin is silent, but one likes to think it is simply waiting to emerge in a better world. If a poet wrote this one line, and never wrote another word, he would deserve to be anthologized.

In "Russian Movie," a complex indictment of fascism and paean to the child's path to adulthood, kites float through the poem like joy.

> The air is filled with kites
> and ancient knowledge and you see hands
> rising everywhere trying to grasp clouds…

While the kites don't rise forever, they do fly. I have flown kites with André de Korvin, and he smiles still.

In de Korvin's fantastical world, the perennial outsiders and lost souls are "wounded angels," each in his own way. The poet is a "one winged angel" who does not surrender. The one winged angel survives, like de Korvin himself survived a childhood in Nazi-occupied Paris, to bear witness. The one winged angel persists, tells his tales, sheds glimmers of enlightenment – dreams on.

De Korvin's work is positively Joycean in its richness and density. These poems are a strong potion in which dramatic personal history, major world events, incisive social commentary and a unique world view collide to create a mind landscape of original thought, bouquets of striking images and small epiphanies that will stay with the reader a long time. *A One Winged Angel* is a museum-worthy tapestry of poetry.

Introduction

We were the only remaining passengers, the alien and I. The bus had stalled and everyone, even the driver, had left. The alien was reading the Los Angeles Times while puffing on a frayed cigarette. Now and then it would look outside, blow smoke that would slowly curl into large O's. Mentally, I kept adding n and e after each smoky O so I imagined the word One, a kind of halo or message perpetually hovering over that odd shaped head.

Its left wing was resting, at an awkward angle, against the back of the seat. The right one was missing. The creature looked like a one winged angel that had seen better days. I noticed how white its face was. *It has swallowed so much salt during its stay on our planet because it ate the bitterness of our world* ran through my mind.

I had seen it in the past. It had no wing then. The first time was in a movie theater. There was a huge white statue looming at the entrance. When the wind picked up and blew at just the right angle, the statue started to speak. I couldn't understand what it was saying. A few of the words sounded like salt… weeds.

Again, I gazed at the white face and smoky halos. Suddenly it looked up and caught my stare. For a brief instant I thought I saw miles of rails running in the depth of its eyes. *Where are they running to?* I wanted to ask. *To revolutions* it said with a smile.

Many years went by before I came across another angel. It had two large wings and almond shaped eyes. Later, I learned it had flown all the way from China.

Today Yi is my wife and I dedicate this book to her as we travel to the many revolutions of our lives.

We all rise to reach our spiritual selves. Not being perfect, sooner or later we fall. After each fall, we strive to rise again. Humanity has always been on that cycle of rising and falling. If real angels have two wings and a human face, then every human attempting to soar starts to look more and more like A One Winged Angel.

I One

IRS

The committee's position is that clouds
moving across state lines
do so with intent to evade and
the sun in the red and clouds in the black

create taxable events says the agent.
When I start to speak,
he puts a burning coal on my tongue.
I dream of autumn, falling leaves,

corn fields stretching wide
and trees bending slowly
under a cold and scheming sky.
Clouds start to ponder

their next winning move.
A white castle enters a black queen,
part of her face drifts in the wind.
I want to hide in my room,

my head turned away from the window
so as not to see the queen's torn face
slowly flowing East.
Many nights I lie awake,

committee members come knocking on my door
sparks fly from their hoof-shaped hands,
equine faces half hidden under dark hats.
I move from square room to square room.

I'd like to sit forgotten on some Ferris wheel,
my feet 100 feet above ground.
I don't want an army of lawyers,
I just want to be lucky although

I'm now charged with pushing luck.
I whisper over and over
The committee's position is that clouds
moving across state lines...

When I leave, I pay
ten years of deadman walking,
five miles of borrowed dreams
and the change I get is

one night sinking in my coffee cup,
two winds mumbling a bad Russian poem
and half a rainbow streaming down
my window's myopic eye.

Handshake

There's a kind of desperation
about her, nothing specific, just
a feeling that

the most minor
occurrence would
topple her

life. The walls
in her room are gloomy
green. She stays

home all day.
It's so hard to meet people
in the suburbs

and hard to walk up
to someone's door and
knock. Often in her dreams

she opens door
after door, surprised
to feel rain

embracing her and
gliding across
long empty rooms

and the wind
cold and silent
shaking her hand.

Guilt

Traveling from cities to cities
and countries to countries,
we sought other jails.
We ignored prisons that didn't have
the most lethal reputations.
There was no need to go through
all that red tape to get arrested.

We could just walk in
and demand to be judged.
The judges weren't much on talking
and would hand out
the harshest sentence.

We were all torn up inside,
you know what I mean?
We didn't ask for
what was happening.
It was those crazy days,
small pieces of a puzzle
that never made sense.

Some of us were sentenced
to death by living,
others just sat there in limbo.
Those who died watched the living
wait for Monday, Tuesday, Wednesday

and then Thursday, Friday
and Saturday and Sunday
so they could start again,
at the end of the week
to wait for Monday, Tuesday,
you know what I mean?
Those long processions of days
dressed in dark, awkward

like employees of a funeral home
on their way to the burial
of a wealthy client,
all of a sudden realizing
they had lost their way.

Breakdown

There was a ball of pain
that was building up
and when you pulled a thread,
everything started to unwind,
everything came undone.

The threads were not disconnected,
they were part of the same large ball.
Your heart was ready to go nova
imploding into all you had
ignored for many years.

When the police broke into your apartment,
they found you prone on the black
linoleum not knowing who you were
and the phone swinging off its hook,
a metronome saying no to harmony.

Heartbreak had moved from your eyes
to your whole body.
Your relatives hoped you would smile
that your breakdown would be
like that of a car, requiring

a minor switch in thinking,
a quick change of heart,
a small repair bill,
and they would drive you
away, good as new.

The Sentence

The times were against you,
the times and these books
telling all of us who didn't fit
what we should do.

You searched for words, feeling words
somehow had the power to save you
and fog shrouded your stanzas,
the abyss of pages showing through black print.

There were more people on earth
than in the whole history of man.
Phones whispered to reach out and touch,
to listen and hear that pin drop.

You were told loneliness wasn't a problem
and the country was filled with stores where
every kind of relationship was sold.
When you got there, though

the stores were empty.
You kept praying, and still
you couldn't tune people in and
out in rhythm with changing times.

You became exhausted, dragging
your tundra wherever you went.
You took a pistol and fired, hoping to kill
winter that wouldn't leave your head.

Your wound opened, a large O and your body
uncoiled, an exclamation mark
at the end of a harsh sentence, telling it,
O yes telling it like it really was!

Novocain

The dentist's face pulls
darkness into the lamp's light.
I think of the eclipse of the sun.

My tongue lies still in my mouth.
He tells me large visions always
bring the aches of losses

and taste of ashes to our lips.
When dreams fall, we hide them
under pillows of wishful thinking

waiting for the sandman to take all.
Yet, he says, we go sleepwalking
on rooftops of imagined cities,

unstable structures made of cards,
dreaming queens of diamond,
dreaming kings of heart.

When we wake, we open our mouths
to spit copper coins, small change
to make the down payment

for guilt ridden moments, for
words spoken without passion, for
letters we never wrote, for

angels gunned down somewhere
in bad places of our hearts,
their deaths a paleness on that green door

we sense slowly closing
in some dream we can't even
remember at dawn.

An Autumn Sunset

You sit beside a dead phone,
trying hard to remember.
The metaphors of disconnection emerge,
calling from a distant past

the future's unlisted years.
You enter a country so strange
that strangeness becomes lethal.
A different season invades your room.

You pick up a handful of dead leaves,
trying to read your sentence,
scribbled by some overworked judge,
in Cyrillic-like letters, on the dark

decaying surface of autumn.
Never leaving your room, you enter
a country where calls are never returned,
petitions reach the wrong officials,

credit cards carry the serial number
of your expiration day.
The strangeness becomes lethal.
The rise of monetary values signals

the fall of every dream's worth.
You sit beside a dead phone,
looking through yellow pages,
trying hard to remember. Autumn

leaves drift through your room.
A wounded sky stumbles
and falls, bruised and
bloodied by the evening sun.

Thunderstorm

You felt the hot breath of the sky
and memories went up in smoke
from overheated rooftops, went

rising from parking lots, overrun
by acres and acres of marigolds,
ascended from hoods of old cars

sold at half price by repo men.
The sun flexed its multi-mile legs
and the world caught fire.

Headlines kept rolling, exiting
the dark print of pages, speeding
over memory lanes of passersby.

All the earth's bitterness hovering,
a quiet haze over loud blues
played in neighborhood bars.

World news turning a corner, inept clocks
trying hard to translate time,
worn down buses slowing down

zig zagging their way
to the nearest stop, parking
out of traffic's way.

People in the rain passing by
like deported tomorrows
and the future turning to stare

at you with its pale eyes.
You, just standing there, oblivious
to the cool applause of the rain.

Perspectives

4 pm. His shadow moving like a wave,
breaking at right angles on each wall,
stepping over sunny pools concealing
the harsh lessons of concrete.

It was rumored to be born from an eclipse,
the one featured in the two hour show,
unfolding under a starry sky stretched taut
over the streets of his hometown.

Now taller than the local TV tower,
it had already forgotten
the very humble beginnings:
two square feet of cloudy vision

on a doormat slowly losing its thread.
7 pm, the upper part of its body
became disconnected from its feet.
The curb went black where he walked.

8 p.m. changes started to flow
from the hard surface of pavements.
A nod and parts of its body went rolling
amidst cars, houses, and the corner bank.

He was a self made man,
proud of his fortune and fame,
didn't want 8:30 pm to be there,
8:30 with the sun sliding across roofs.

Although he was suing time
for reckless speeding, night
was already speeding through
the suburbs of Tomorrow.

He died at 8:45 pm near the stop
sign at Fate and Loss.
Some swear they saw long shadows
veil the pale face of the moon.

The flower shop is open 24 hrs a day.
Inside, silence sticks to the walls like ivy.
In my hand sunflowers write
yellow stanzas in the night.

Obituary

Imagine a narrow road circling
a gas station at the edge of the sky
and newspapers unfolding their wings
to rise over rooftops of the world.

Remember your lost home. Lying on your back
watch clouds shape faces you once knew and
leaves missing you by inches, whisper in your ear
premonitions of war in Autumn's broken Latin.

Feel July leaving your eyelids and
December fall from your mouth
like the copper coins you used to spit when
daydreaming you called departed friends.

A Russian wind mumbles poorly written verses
and you hear rain walking,
a high-heeled woman of ill repute
on the pavement of your hometown.

Her cigarette lights up the sky and
what you once were explodes
and comes down in burning pieces,
falling through lists of the dead, your ashes
slowly settling into print.

Continuous Performance

They throw flowers into your grave
and you throw them back.
Colors explode over tombstones
and friends go home, blues, reds
and yellows pressed against their chests.

Last cigarette, says the man and
he blows smoke high into the air.
Clouds drift over the city, a poem
loiters in a deserted parking lot.
Smoke curls into an open mouth.

Smoke says: *in my recurrent dream,*
the world rises in silent circles.
Faint heartbeats echo coins fallen
from the pockets of the homeless
living at the edge of borrowed time.

A train runs behind your closed eyelids,
it picks up speed and people become dots,
the end of a hard to follow novel printed
on a horizon too distant to read and
steam draws ghosts of departed friends.

You rewind your life like a film,
waiting for bright lights to flicker
in a dark and crowded room, waiting
for the movie to start over, hoping
now and then, for a different rerun.

II Winged

Writer's Block

There were many people
on this odd street
that didn't seem to end and

changed names so many times,
it was real easy
to get lost.

A passerby had thrown away
a painting of some bridge, the river below
washed away with time.

The man selling roasted chestnuts was sad.
He didn't understand why he sold
chestnuts on this strange street.

He thought he always wanted to be
a philosopher, maybe living
under a bridge, thinking deep thoughts.

Only there was no bridge,
the only bridge was in the painting
fading away to just an arc.

Faded like the memories
the man had of chestnut trees
waving from Parisian streets,

glimpsed on a postcard,
long ago, when he had moved
far from his hometown.

I write a poem about losses
and all the objects of my grief
freeze inside my pen,

as if the pen, suddenly alive,
its transparent heart showing
almost empty, was trying to stop

blue memories from spilling over
that long white world and was
holding on to everything it had.

The Blue Chevy

Rain. Radio weeps
inside the beaten Chevy.
Pershing Square high rise,
invisible behind fogged glass.

Windshield wipers moving,
long fingers trying to grasp night.
News and music wailing and
streets curving around the future

as someone's hand erases
pieces of yesterday on the fog
shrouded glass and unthinking
rain washes out

memories and lanes to
what was a borrowed life.
The Chevy slip sliding
over no name streets

miles and years clicking
on the low lit dial, as if
lost on Regret Drive it wanted
to focus on everything

that makes a Chevy blue.
The sky's so worn out
it can't remember
half of its stars.

I Always Wanted

To write a poem where rivers flow
free as my verse
and high rises drown in purple

and gold waves of the sun.
Always wanted to write a poem
where children shape

smiling faces in the mud.
A poem where weeping willows
shake their green heads, cheerfully

gazing into the deep
hazy mirror of the sky.
Sipping coffee, I look

through my many windows
and wait for a poem
to drive by.

Although sunlight is everywhere
and moody cups throw halos
like saints handing in their resignation,

street lights bow their heads,
their eyes scanning every direction
hoping for night to come soon.

I drink my coffee black,
and lean over the white table
and although the room

is brightly lit,
my head fills up
with missing stanzas,

and throws starless nights
across that white table,
across the crumpled pages of my draft.

Microcosm

At first rain traced one line poems
like that professor, trying hard to earn tenure,
publishing one liners by Russian poets.

Rain though didn't scribble Russian, Spanish
or Chinese. It tried to write polyglot
like those clocks in Saint Lazare station

whispering time in no matter what language.
Later, it began to jot down paragraphs
about the sky in Paris

London and Rome
really being the same sky,
a blank piece of paper to write on.

Inspired, it filled space with lines
running in all directions
as if written by a dyslexic child, scribbling

huge letters in a notebook way too small.
Frustrated, it wrote longer and longer poems
like that graphomaniac admiral

practicing epic prose on rainy weekends.
Later still, the sun came for a while
and penciled red, most of rain's stanzas

miming that editor, anxious to show
to every beginning poet the real
horror of mixed metaphors.

I write about the heart's dark alleys
and the lamp leans over my shoulder,
angry angel glaring at my lines.

Last Week's Movie

When night falls
and mirrors become lazy
refusing to reflect

and hallucinations walk right up
to the doors of the movie
house long deserted

like ghosts of Parisian prostitutes
with golden hearts
and dreams exit through open windows

to collide in empty streets,
forming a pulsing line marking
the boundaries of a world some call

the aura of our planet, that's when
the corner gas lamp flickers, on
and off and on and off as if

standing motionless all day
it had suddenly started to shake
and unable to stop

had become vulnerable
like a little girl, as if
leaning over the dark asphalt

it had seen the ghost
of the Power Co. rise,
everything lit for just a second,

and was weeping brightness
through its Cyclops eye
somehow shrinking in despair,

somehow twisting like a flower.
Sadness of last week's movie
raining on our street.

And The Reason

for all of it can be found
where gas lamps dim over faraway
fields of withered corn and air conditioners
never cease complaining to third rate clerks
about the amnesia of empty coats
lying in waiting rooms of small
railway stations.

You ask why people die,
disappear from your life,
and the reason is the absence of future
hanging over the birth of objects,
pushing them into bottomless years,
seducing time to mimic parking lots
veiled in acres of marigolds.

The reason is absence hanging
over lost coins waiting
to be picked up
just for luck.
People die and the void
their departure creates turns to music
taking leave of violins.

Late at night, sorrow enters our homes
tip-toes on the linoleum of poorly lit kitchens
and reasons go bump against nights,
turn unstable like
that brooding countess exiled
among the sad notes of music,
unstable like a song

half recognized and then fading
in the static of an old radio,
slowly hummed out of existence, unstable
like that cat smiling at everything
until nothing remains except the smile
and words departing slowly
from the silence of our lips.

Sketching a French Poem.

Mannequins wear Mona Lisa smiles,
their heads held high above unruly years.
Their eyes reflect nothing or perhaps signal
it's now your show.

He pushes La Gare St. Lazare
With all of its clocks
and also the color of his mother's eyes
right onto the sky which mockingly kept

staring down at him, the sky
refusing to wear any color, except
the color of his mother's eyes.
The sky, now allowing a small cloud

to wrap itself around the Sunoco building
like a shawl around the shoulders of a woman
suddenly feeling her age.
Mannequins, mouths wide open,

seem on the verge of saying something
or perhaps on the verge of reading
poems of love and destruction as they leave
their place of work, although it's not yet five.

They walk out, afraid of these clocks,
these clouds, the color of his mother's eyes
and later that sunset which just might
cut the sky like razor blades.

Passages

Long after music crossed 12th
and Main and long after
some of its echoes jumped over
walls of poor neighborhoods

or simply put: long after music came
and left, Sunday started walking
toward Monday. It was evening so
its dark hair swept the curbs.

Absent minded passersby thought
they saw the sun going down
a bit early, slowly warping
and then erasing all shadows.

In this late hour, if you really listen
you'll hear yourself talk in your sleep,
sentences turning slow and awkward
when you remember all that fog

surrounding the many high
and low points of your life while the moon
quietly ticks, its face breaking into pieces,
drifting through your window screen, recording

earth's uncertain path. Awake you wonder
what deity passing by shredded time
into small silver coins and carelessly threw them
on the rough surface of your floor.

Long Sleep Motel

Time drew circles the day I rented
a room in Long Sleep Motel. I lie in my bed, writing
24 hours a day and wherever stanzas take me, the bed's desert
blows sand in my eyes. Wherever I go, I drag
long roads of regrets and winding streets of time lost.
Years twist into knots, months burn blacker
and thoughts stall, like traffic
at 5 o'clock in a town all of a sudden
self conscious of its age.

I lie in my star-shaped bed,
jab a rusted pen
deep into my bruised veins.
Ink flows inside my body.
Why do you write, people have asked,
To die and live, I would answer.
My blood is bluer than Gauloise Bleue smoke
that would curl into a ? on my dead father's lips,
blue like the four motel clerks

all dressed in black uniforms
bought years ago when working
across the street, at Heart Break Motel.
Management gave them pink slips when they went on strike
for higher wages and better heart insurance.
These days, they stand by the main gate,
angel wings huge behind their backs
and lazy weekend drivers mistake them
for palms with broken branches.

In my room, the moon clones itself over
and over on the pastel walls.
That same moon running
non-stop from floor to ceiling,
cut off at its high and low points,

like the first woman I loved, her memory running
across blue painted years,
her face growing hazy
at happy and sad points of our lives.

Ink travels deep inside my body,
distorts every object in the room.
Faucets weep, one tear at a time
over the abyss of the sink.
Stern mirrors glare, shining
their cold lights over
the many versions of my life
and when my head hits the pillow, I lie motionless
traveling not in distance but in depth.

The bed's desert follows me, stretching further
any sleepless eye can see.
Gold sand, red sun
rising from my blanket
and mirages roam like scarlet fever
once roamed my room,
swinging its hips, dressed in red
pressing hard against my eight year old body,
a street walker with a loaded gun.

My eyes are two ink blots and ink
runs over the wall paper moons.
My Armenian math teacher
holding a watch in the palm of his hand,
leaps over the last day of his life
to be one minute by my side.
Trying to pull me back in time,
he draws circles on my bedroom walls.
Waving his pen, pacing back and forth,

he asks his unruly students
to sketch in their blue books
the shortest path to misfortune.
He moves his arms, his sleeves painting
the twisted wings of a bird shot by hunters
trigger happy with their new shotguns.

Trying hard for an A, I write
The shortest path to misfortune
is exile's longest path.

The classroom fades and the lesson lives
in the depth of parallel lines
running across a painted sky,
parallel like exile's many paths
curving around what was lost,
intersecting misfortune at every turn.
The wind weeps when it confesses:
for a long time it kept blowing
wavy lines and broken circles in the sand.

With every heartbeat, ink races through my body.
Beat-- I remember new republics
sliding across the dark windows of a bus,
blue Chevrolets running on empty,
dented like metaphysics,
my father boarding the train rolling over
the one way bridge of Coma river.
In the station of nowhere, rails screaming
louder than women giving birth.

IRS agents dreaming ashes
piling up on Wall Street.
Beat-- I remember the blue hat dreamer
handcuffed by Soho policemen
and a midnight sun bouncing off
adult bookstores and nostalgia rising
through ventilators of empty restaurants,
stadium men swimming in metal rivers
and Bonaparte's galaxy hat floating

across my dreams of Chinatown.
Beat-- I remember war time weekends
with their displays of tin politicians
covered with confetti, the color of blood,
the orange-haired general,
a single eye lighting up his face,
river boats departing for yesterday
and military music lingering in schoolyards
long after the troops had left.

The bedroom clock chimes *Guilty*,
its dial stares into space,
luminous, like a girl's face, as time
stands still after her first kiss.
Street lights come marching in
with night still wrapped around their necks
and Berlin wall floats by with its moon
pale as aspirin, its myopic moon
seeing deep but unable to see far.

Wherever stanzas take me, the bed's desert
slowly settles like a blanket.
I wait for the future
to come marching in.
I wait for a parade of events so astonishing,
every grain of sand will be night.
I wait for a parade of hours so monumental,
my moons will open their mouths and whistle
at women strolling past blue years.

In my parade, oil and vinegar will mix
and form a rainbow of colors
and that rainbow will be sentences
flowing out from politician's mouths.
In my parade, the sadness of sycamores
will be studied in every university
and in every motel
the abyss of sinks will be filled
with more butterflies than Nabokov's novels.

Dollar bills will turn brown
because they would think of themselves
as green leaves and would think of time
as a river bringing autumn
and autumn will be an aging man
sitting in his boat and slowly rethinking
the whole concept of gravity
and gravity would go on vacation
so everything heavy would become light.

In my parade, Death would wake up
and forgetting her amnesia,
she would recognize her cousin Sleep.
Death and Sleep would tip-toe
so as not to wake the dead and the sleeping
and reaching for the stars,
they would bend over every dreamer,
lighting up their faces in the night
and night would smile like a woman in love.

The bed's desert which had followed me
from stanza to stanza
would be lost in my parade
and planet earth would not be headed
wherever we all think it's headed.
The known universe would be expanding
across many universes of stanzas
so we would inadvertently inhale poems like smoke
my father inhaled from his Gauloise Bleue.

In my parade, Gauloise Bleue smoke
would form the outline of a blue castle
and entering that castle, I would read
postcards from gravity still on vacation
so scales would imagine me
to be smoke of departing trains.
Departing, I would wave from my window
watching Long Sleep recede, a dot
in the Tundra of Great Horizons.

My eyes all focused, not on distance but on depth
on the smoke of Gauloise Bleue, curling
as if it was trying to put ??
at the end of words, words of departure
hanging over the meaning of things, so many words
the cyclical devaluation of dreams deports them
to places where pale horses graze lists of the missing
and sometimes, when we remember deep,
foreign words assemble in our private cities.

Walking in the rain we desperately cling
to torn umbrellas showing
broken skies over our heads and
a harsh alien wind tries hard
to say in its own words *a violin sleeps*
in the aching heart of every rose.
Long sleep, bringing a different grammar
to the language of flowers
and mute things.

Driving Through A Foggy Intersection In Poem City

Mid 50's. St. Lambert Street.
I lay my head on the kitchen table
half closing my eyes.

The wine bottle looms blacker
than the factory building
I will pass each day.

The salt shaker shimmers, a pale angel,
the sun forming halos on white powder
and the radio whispers news of the world.

If the wine would spill on the table
if the wind would blow on the salt
there would be dark rivers and white clouds.

The kitchen clock would then
start running back,
like the St Lazare clocks in one of my poems.

Sometimes poems take you back
to different times and places,
to the mid 50's, to St Lambert Street.

Sometimes places and times take you back
to poems you wrote
like you being vapor rising

slowly in your mother's dream.
You drive, not really knowing
where you are

in Poem City, looking for
the birthplace of your stanzas
and through black ink and white pages

you see salt in the eyes of angels
and discarded images bleeding
words darker than wine.

Frenchman Sleeping In Texas

He sleeps. Monday stares
with its muddy eyes at the bedroom
mirror, Monday with its white lips,
swaying like a web in the morning

wind. In the tarnished glass, three-
legged chairs show their age,
leaning as if they were three
centuries old. He dreams, his head

almost divorced from its pillow
and the room sensing
the strange geography of his vision
grows silent. A city rises behind

his closed eyelids and
his breath deposits poems
on the pale ceiling of the room.
Gas lamps loom taller than

the Eiffel tower, almost
airborne when he remembers
how the Parisian sky was
when he was young.

Ah, Apollinaire

Je m'en allais sur le bord de la Seine
Yes, I was going Buffalo Bayou's way,

un livre ancient sous le bras,
an old book under my arm,
an old book whose words
no longer made sense.

Le fleuve est pareil a ma peine,
bayou waters drown the streets
where my poems wander,

il coule et ne tarit pas.
and ink runs over
the high points of my life
staining them blue.

Quand donc finira la semaine?
Running over muddy waters
an eastern wind scribbles
poems of war, emigration
and fatal wounds, stanzas
flowing up and down
like broken waves.

III Angel

When Mr. Blues Meets an East European

He doesn't hum tunes watching
that evening sun go down, he doesn't dream
Southern bells ringing or cotton fields
with farmers knee-deep in mud.

He doesn't talk about the homeless
starving in New Orleans or New York.
No, Mr. Blues is silent. He stares
with his eyes of Pole shot in Chicago,

his eyes of East German lost in New Berlin,
his eyes of Ukrainian dreaming KGB,
his eyes of Serbian murdered in his sleep,
his eyes of raped women, of grieving widows,

his eyes of orphaned Azerbaijani,
his eyes of dead horse pushed
by his master stumbling
with a broken down cart through

shrapnel raining on nowhere street,
his eyes of Russian soldier
stranded in some bombed out
far away village in Chechnya.

Exploding places, exploding homes.
Mr. Blues walking all over the planet,
sometimes inhaling silence through his sax,
sometimes spilling music through his eyes.

Looking For Nancy

You desperately hugging Nancy
at the doorway of that old hotel,
telling her she looks like

a million dollars and cancer
can be beat and who knows
what tomorrow might bring.

The hotel watches the future
roll past its windows and already
you hold absence in your arms.

The parking lot to be built
next year is now the death
dream of condemned buildings.

Later, Nancy coming down
as memory mixed with drizzle,
hovering over passing cars and drivers

blind to angels loitering on Main.
The office clock unable to register
the true passage of time.

Shutting your eyes you watch
the city of your poems break apart,
words coming down awkward,

the sky all of a sudden a stranger,
as if it wanted no more
to be part of things

and suddenly air-borne, amazed
you watch Nancy miming
a lone gliding cloud.

Expanding Universes

In this street, black curtains blocked
the vision of windows
so no single building could grasp

the magnitude of that new beginning.
No single building could feel
the long line of cardboard angels

and loneliness became a new minted coin.
Every stone falling
from the eyes of three winged birds echoed

weeks fallen from the pockets of the homeless.
Windows became afflicted with blindness
on account of monochrome thinking while

clocks were running into the red and green of time.
Things did not become simple however
because time was color blind

and so was wanted for reckless driving.
The rooster crowed its alarm
but was booed by military trumpets

who thought alarms were for sissies.
Behind glass, the blue eyes of dolls
couldn't reflect the fire of life

so ashes covered the inner eyes of sleepless men.
Black letters on white paper
tried to go on strike invoking

too much greed in the Sunday ads.
A and Z got up and marched off the pages
their political discourse taking on the sound of bees,

though letters in the middle refused to rock the boat.
Crazy thoughts crossed the minds of discarded objects
although some said the objects

weren't so much discarded as defective.
Their thoughts, anyway, formed a pattern
that mimed a cross-word puzzle

where the key sentence was: *the sadness of sycamores.*
I lie in my bed, trying to catch
light behind black curtains,

thick sheets of salt cover my eyes.
To stay awake I recite my mantra
to every metal conveying emotion like

the hatred of lead, the deviousness of copper.
I think of my father moving in space, his laughter
the color of zinc in his lighter moments

the color of gold when he concentrates.
It was on account of black curtains, sneaky
new philosophies started to parade

spitting cherry pits wherever they went.
Garbage cans pouted, good citizens
they felt cherry pits were theirs for the taking

as they watched pits pass them by like planets.
Thick sheets of salt cover my eyes
and I dream of lakes, their waters

blazing brighter than liquid metals.
Although loneliness was a new minted coin
prices of bygone days went through the roof

$ signs exploding from every building.
Heat wave moved into that street
and $ signs rose up like vapor

only to rain later for many days.
Rusty bicycles watched new cycles
become immutable laws

$ signs raining then turning to vapor only to rain again.
Objects that were not discarded began to be seduced
by separatist ideas like tires rolling away

from cars as they remembered their rubbery past.
Later, coffee didn't want to rest
in void spaces of the cups so

it pushed hard to gain night status.
Doors walked away from buildings, claiming
their birthright to open up

to the flow of new ideas.
Black curtains opted to remain
side by side with windows

not for brotherly love but for protection.
One saw many weddings between
what once was at opposite

poles of comprehension.
Grooms, bleeding gasoline as they went to war,
brides, prayers falling as Tundra from their lips

and the priest, a door wide open in space.
My eyes are covered with thick sheets of salt
and I repeat my mantra, addressed

to the power of iron, the beauty of chrome.
The sky, everyday tried a little harder
to lay parallel to the street

who didn't think it was funny.
To retaliate it grew potholes
to show the sky how ugly

its behavior really was these days.
It was spring, so cardboard angels
slowly became lawyers

small wings visible under expensive suits.
Sycamore trees, formed a forest
in the predictable nightmares of judges,

judges with sand running down their eyes.
Black curtains covered the eyes of justice
and when a plague of frogs fell on the city court

no amount of kissing made them prince.
The real princes were sleeping on asphalt
in railway stations, in glass factories,

poems coming out as flames from their open mouths.
At times I dream of my mother
and my sleep deposits

blue paint on my cracked ceiling.
Although loneliness was a new minted coin
the rise and fall and rise and fall of the $ sign

glued inflation on the price of defunct things.
I pay five days of loneliness
for three days of light and the change I get is

one stone fallen from the eye of the three winged bird.
Although my eyes are covered with thick sheets of salt
I see my father rising from the sadness of sycamores,

soaring from the depth of every color.
He speaks and his words put gold
on every roof of this street, put

gold on a horse that happens to be there.
The horse rears, its head blots out the sun and it spits
broken violins wrapped in unreadable stanzas

so for hours I hum a half forgotten tune.
At night the downtown bridge
sings to passing cars and I think of stars

slowly moving through space.
The bridge sings lines
from my father's poem

and I can't tell if it's gold
or music that comes
tumbling from its lights.

Giving It All Away

You put your eyes down
on that long winding road and
surprised, the sun stumbles and falls.
Evening rises, firing
light against unmoving
armies of fresh- painted signs.

The stars have walked
away from this night
slamming hard every door
and because of this
your bones are white
with the bitterness of separation

and silence of deserted homes.
You leave your lips
further down the road.
They sing the sadness of sycamores
and the autumn wind sweeps away
unsaid words from your lungs.

Your lungs are trees
bending over the red
rivers of your heart
so when the wind blows
you hear every loss
flowing through your veins.

Your heart whispering words
with that heavy Slavic accent, your heart
a living map of Russia, sometimes
miming poems of hunger and
war sprayed on brick walls
in bad neighborhoods.

You throw your poems on the courthouse steps
and the sea of justice carries them away,
your stanzas drifting past seven foot flowers
opening and closing like robes of judges,
their roots running deep into the corroded
soil of submerged corporations.

You lose what you love
in the wasteland of cheap possessions
as if the lines you wrote were
not coming down as poet blood
but were lines of houses rising
amidst fields of your hometown.

Stanzas learned and forgotten like music
gracefully taking leave of violins.
Your lines keep on dancing,
one step forward, two steps back,
and when you hum, they sway
and turn on the road in time.

Metamorphosis

All morning, his lawnmower rides through
the despair of grass and marigolds.
Later, I ask the man what he's planting.
A heavy accent obscures his reply,
salt and weeds, I imagine,
he says in his strange language.

When I look up he looms,
a huge white statue, the kind
that stands in front of movie theaters,
left arm dragging like a chain.
Old age isn't what you think.
The distance from his room to the porch
grows wider each week.

At times, the man stands motionless
as if turning to salt.
The wind deposits words on his lips.
I listen, rough sentences rolling
not bound to any tongue or grammar.
The tempo of his speech alien as if

the bronze horse downtown was
talking to the stars and
moved by the cadence of its words
had started to neigh all the music
it held deep in its heart
because rhythm had become
more important than words.

The University

U smiles in the dark,
an untenured instructor ready to quiz night.
The first question is :
A Hispanic janitor takes the slow running elevator,
sinking to a depth beyond comprehension,
deeper than one thousand Ophelias drowning
in lit 101, the life lines of her hands trace
entry roads to new continents.
Please answer : How many failures
can you read in her eyes?

1 a.m. Madeline types another memo :
Mr President, we the faculty want to express
60% dissatisfaction with leaves of absence
and blank pages scattered across desks outline
the multiple faces of misfortune, crumpled pages cry out
the sad list of the unpublished, the tragic list of the perished,
lecturers whose contract is not renewed,
assistant professors denied tenure,
tenured professors paving their lives with questions
and answers neatly typed on unread manuscripts.

U smiles in the dark and winks dirty windows
at the prison, its macho neighbor,
bricks running down its walls like blood.
In her dreams, Madeline sees the Merrill Lynch Bull
crossing the bridge, money
slowly shifting from university to prison.
She types : *Legislators, we want you to stop*
these money transfers away from education
and awake she wonders why
the Merrill Lynch Bull never goes the other way.

I grew up poor on the left
bank of River War.
River War with its one-way bridges running
to poverty, to depression, to wasted lives.
The stock market would rise and fall
like the blood pressure of some terminally ill patient
and history, eyes hot with fever

wept widows into morning trains.
River War pushing orphans, broken cities
and people who could never change, right into our future.

We stood outside school
holding bricks in our hands.
We wanted to stone the police
the teachers, all past French presidents.
We wanted to set history ablaze
and hurl rocks at metaphysics.
So we just stood there, clenching our fists,
scared of going to prison, scared of coming home,
too tired to hurl anything
at the dull distant sky.

I wanted to understand time,
to hold time, so days and nights
would stop crossing one-way bridges
like cattle headed for the slaughter house.
I wanted to lay my body down
across the pavements of our world
to stop so many good people
walking away and never coming back.
I dreamed giant pendulums
swinging and missing me by inches.

I dreamed endless roads in disrepair
men and women working overtime,
jack-hammers breaking up their lives.
I knew time by what it was not.
It was not solitary diamonds
circling the fingers of rich women,
nor the moon, soccer ball
kicked, rolling and bouncing through
the playground of forgotten gods,
an endless field with no goal posts.

We search for time while it slips
between our fingers like sand,
like daylight slowly slips away
when night comes sailing in

and paints the sky navy blue. When evening comes,
we cover our private time and space with faces
we once knew. We listen to voices growing faint
like the sound of bees swarming in a distant field.
The perished inhabit our landscapes and when the dead speak
their words sink into the deep fissures of our hearts.

Legislators, we want you to stop
these transfers away from our rights.
We want to express unhappiness with these leaves of absence,
taking away so many good people so soon.
We want you to stop these transfers
away from human comprehension.
We want you to stop building
that thick wall of time running
between what we love and what we miss,
between what some of us are and some of us were.

Madeline types another memo and I
lean across empty years, trying to remember
what the president looked like in old pictures I once saw.
I try to imagine what he looks like, after so many years
and question marks fill my field of vision.
I try to understand where he comes from
and endless computations darken my pages.
I ask my colleagues who among them has seen him.
No one has. He's rumored to be
here, there, everywhere.

I walk the halls, searching
looking into every classroom on every floor.
Rumors say he fills
the whole space with light,
his halo glowing 24 hours each day,
brighter than a 60 watt bulb.
I want to tell him U isn't doing
all that well. I want to tell him thousands and
thousands are flunking out their lives and
happiness retention comes close to dismal failure.

I want to tell him words
running through my mind
when I think of winds blowing
through Harlem like stainless steel blades,
words running when I sit outside
not doing anything, just drinking coffee
with some cream in it, like I once drank nights
whitened by too many stars.
Words running through winter days
when flock of geese darken the sky.

I want to tell him the day will come when
I too will take the slow running elevator
and catch every failure in the janitor's eyes
and on that day her Hispanic eyes will glow
like shards of glass inside some vast kaleidoscope
where structures of new universes unfold.
We will rise higher than the highest floor
lighter than air, over the bayou that runs
many miles around the prison. Free at last we'll hail
fast moving clouds with star-shaped hands.

Height and Depth

You bright windows of pretty churches,
we dull concrete in poor neighborhoods.
You music, you rhythm
you fireworks, you now.

We tuning out, we absence,
we shadows on the wall.
You crowds, you fast
you pink sunglasses.

We one, we geological time
we granite eyes.
You right words, you smooth
you flower-speak.

We awkward, we lethal images
we tundra-words.
You higher and higher
in public opinion.

We deeper and deeper
in private grief.
You lighter than air,
you registering on no scale.

We heavier than a millennium,
sinking where we stand.

We Lost Our Way

6 am. Clouds already graying
line up, three miles long,
shifting in the rising wind,
gloomy immigrants blown

from country to country,
while applying for permanent visas
or hiring lawyers to fight deportation.
Blindfolded justice can't shoot straight

so bullets plow through flesh
like tractor blades cutting open
the parched soil of their homeland.
I walk the streets, watching

the plaza's red flowers fade.
From far away I can hear
the train whistle blow. Later,
the town is silent, and

buses roll away like dreams.
White statues seem to whisper
we lost our way
to the children's park.

Day after day barges drift,
Sundays floating then sinking
in the abyss of bottomless years.
Day after day

illegals move their possessions.
They fade into the sunset,
their shadows dark spots
on the outbound bridge.

This Street Runs

Through the hidden side of your eyelids.
Pershing Square high-rise looms ahead.
It's been night for many years.
The sky sleeps, its stars tightly shut and silence
turns lethal in the nightmare of broken pianos.
The high-rise is many stories high,
some of its windows, always lit.

Idle hours rise from the ashtray.
You watch your life stories
play out, framed in brightly lit windows.
On the first floor, a child running
toward his mother's arms
and on the second, you're sixteen
looking at reflections in a tarnished mirror.

Growing up in Paris, amidst Russians in exile,
getting into trouble at school,
Sacha and you banging with a hammer
on a German grenade to make it go off.
Yura taking up cab-driving,
Natasha running away and the radio
always talking Algerian war.

Waving goodbye to your parents at Orly.
Fog shrouding the plane's windows.
New York skyscrappers standing at attention
and you, entering movie houses on 42nd
like tourists enter Roman churches.
Drinking and talking, half English, half French,
Capitalist Gangsters, Gangsters Capitalistes.

Watching Vietnam war movies
on the 6 o'clock news,
blown up bodies coming home,
in plastic bags. Looking
for good times in bad places,
in smog filled streets of LA,
remembering Paris winding alleys.

Working for ibm, interpreting
rows and rows of numbers
like some fortune teller
trying to predict the next earthquake.
Numbers follow you home.
At night, they point like judges
to the landmarks of your life.

Then there's the strange math of loss and separation.
The multiplication of grief,
the dividends of despair,
the remainder of hope,
the shrinking ratio of future over past
and the widening distance between you
and what you once were.

There's also the long story of the dead,
heavy on the past, uncertain on the future.
Your father continuing to live, but in another realm,
going through buildings, walking on thin air,
smiling as he leaves his pastel coffin,
stepping out from yellow photographs
and seen by crowds of friends, in their sleep.

Snow falling for days and you try to read
what snow flakes are writing.
Frost covered fields are torn pages
from your novel still searching for a hero.
Writing for hours, lost in your own room.
Winter and loneliness hover over Indiana.
This is not LA you say and already…

Indiana shrinking in your rear-view mirror.
Lost in one thousand reflections, you are
the man with mirror-like gestures.
Watching Pampas grass plant anarchy
right next to the corner bank.
Texas heat clings to your body
like memories that won't let go.

You embrace the heat of the sun
like we embrace our lovers
and the weight of all the people
and places you carry
is so great that your world slowly
collapse into what lies
at your very center.

And the weight of all the people
and places you carry
is so great that gravity
traps light and
like a star going nova,
you can only be seen
as dark print on this page.

Your life playing 24 hours a day
across countless stories. The sky
sleeps, all its stars tightly shut.
People and time loiter on the street that runs
through the inner side of your eyelids.
A new day takes shape, half hidden
behind dark windows to be lit.

Running to Dark Waters and White Clouds

When you were ten, you killed time
walking the halls of La Gare St. Lazare,
running back and forth
through La Salle des Pas Perdus,
feeling lost amid the station's clocks,
their hands pointing to void spaces in-between hours.
Today, tricking your mind, clocks run counter
clock wise, their revolution erasing our moments.

The future stares through unlit windows,
invisible behind drawn shades
and night evicting sleep watches
the blurred parts of your life
bringing haze to brightly lit rooms.
Pershing Square Hotel floats by,
pulling itself free from the gravity
of French railway stations.

The weight of all the people
and places you carry
is suddenly lighter than
one firebird's feather
so your heart inflates
larger than a helium balloon.
The weight of all the people
and places you carry

is suddenly lighter than
one third of a humming bird song
so your laughter unzips the sky
and you can only
remember the sun
when you think of past lovers.
It's like running through
all your reflections

still lingering in places
and times where you lived.
Intervals of time are shattered
into such unequal lengths,
that ghosts rising from your calculus book,
working their way back,
produce the disintegration
of a made-up life.

Numbers swarm around you, vast and changing,
a flock of hungry blackbirds
descending from dead trees surrounding
the decaying bridge of White River.
Numbers and losses are glued to your eyelids,
their stories harsher than LA pavements,
doors of New York banks
or walls of the longest separation.

Strolling through Paris' winding alleys,
you remember the future,
California dreaming shrouded in smog,
your marriage in a Hollywood church,
plastic bags wrapped around
bodies of soldiers headed home
and the 6 o' clock news where
Vietnam movies will be played.

You remember the future,
meaningless conversations,
faces hiding behind bottles of beer,
broken English, broken French:
Prevert ecrit in good poem
je t' aime tant, time temps
temps time, flower fille, so little time
I love you flower girl.

Memories peel away from your body
like Texas summers in an air conditioned room.
Pampas grass goes underground,
a guerilla warfare against commercial renovation.
Buffalo Bayou recedes faster
than a mirror falling from its wall,
rainy Indianapolis settles on your windshield and
water draws handcuffs around your wrists.

You erase your poems,
the paper turning white
over the streets of nowhere towns,
the eraser working its way back
from last word to first word,
like poems running back through your life,
or blankets of snow exposing as they melt
frozen fields, the color of rust.

Rust, the color of your father's eyes
leaving his pink coffin,
walking through acres of dreams,
walls and buildings unable to slow him down,
gravity failing to pin him to this earth.
Time bounces back and forth
between the dead and the living
with the dead leading the score.

You will lean over the future
the same way you lean over
Bayou waters running past your home,
always surprised at what that magic mirror
might reflect from faraway time.
Your college algebra book floats
from the depth of forty years,
the math fuzzy as metaphysics.

Rush hour traffic on memory lane.
Earlier or was it later,
time bled roses
right next to German tanks.
The corpses of your friends go by
on the river of your dreaming
Sergei, Albert, and Natasha, one day,
stepping through the doors of oblivion.

You're ten and you're running
through the halls of St. Lazare,
through La Salle des Pas Perdus.
The real riddle, a Russian poet wrote, is to find
your own footsteps in the snow.
You're ten and you're running,
your time now showing
on every railway station clock.

Running and there is no St. Lazare.
Church bells, loud as thunder, proclaim
the end of war, the rise of a new dawn.
You hear bombs fall near your school.
 It's Friday the 13 th, everyone is laughing.
You wake, sleep wrapped around your eyes,
you smile, rocked in your mother's arms.
A red moon rises over the hospital crib.

The counter-clock marks 8 pm.
You are one month old.
Thousands of people running,
they will die at the start of war.
War will start in a couple of days.
In between contractions your mother dreams
dark waters and white clouds.
Nazis parade in Berlin.

You are vapor rising in your mother's dream.
You sense the depth of currents, the presence of iron,
electric pulses running through your world,
the transparent film wrapped around your body,
the thin cord that ties you to this planet, you hear
distant echoes of French and Russian conversations.
Over dark waters, below white clouds
you are pure potential, pure possibility.

You are holding on to everything you could be.
You are a blank piece of paper on which
a functionally illiterate war starts to scribble
one more badly written paragraph
university historians will strive to read.
Before, you slept in no space, no time.
Your mother's heartbeats were
songs sung softly just for you.

A Russian Movie

In this late hour, clocks quit being polyglot
and switch instead
to some dialect of time spoken
in different rhythm of minutes.
In this late hour, fires go on strike
and refuse to burn, opting
to mimic the blue hue of ice.
In this late hour, rivers curl like smoke
ready to rise and drown the stars
thinking of them as fish out of water.

You know how late the hour is when you come
to the house of unfocused lights where reflective surfaces
illuminate all directions and torn by conflicting laws of optics
your left thinking goes East, your right dreaming goes West
and your heart beats its separate way. You on memory lane,
at dusk rising from winding rivers,
you absent minded, walking through fires,
moving on roads with no end,
running over dark clouds, all of you
fly apart like pieces of shattered mirrors.

In this late hour, you watch reruns of your life, your life
playing 24 hrs each working day and on weekends too.
The many words you never said
are displayed as closed caption
at the bottom of the screen.
You mumble *show me the path,*
dust rising with every step you take
and the translation reads
he's losing all sense of direction
because gravity's gone.

Dick Stanley and you both thirteen pacing
the streets of a small British town.
The Majestic with Jesus Saves fading on its wall
features two R- rated movies so you ask
all sorts of people to take you in.
You say *We have the money,*
we just need an adult to lead us in.

Dick Stanley and you, banging on the doors of life
and a hot summer sun loiters, a merchant peddling
mirages on a street corner in this small tired town.

The sun rolls red across the screen
(soccer game with God tying the score)
and as it goes by, it turns to ashes
the theater, the mirages and the whole town.
There are only empty fields to stare at
and Stalin rises from the wheat.
Fade in to your parents, pacing back and forth
their small room, somewhere in Paris,
their faces burnt orange like the pages
of their Russian-refugee passports.

Years rise thicker than dust and you remember
Jesus Saves fading on the walls.
You try to hold on to things, to anything
but gravity's gone.
You search for the missing hours
mumbling *where's the path?*
Movies play inside your head
and your parents with their burnt faces
late at night, lean over
the lame dinner table.

Stalin rises from the wheat
and in Sunday school you learn
the tricky geography of Russia,
the fire that rages within
eventually burning sorrow into poems.
In Sunday school you learn
you are mostly made of water
and at night, for hours you try to feel
the direction of your inner currents.
Many lost objects drift in the sea of your body.

You grew up half water and half fire
not having any small spot of earth to claim
and using air only as a canvas to sketch
drowned memories and ideas burned beyond recognition.

You were never good at reading waters, so you kept
writing about rivers in order to grow
and your teacher said this was like
trying to hold absence in your hand
because, in the end, we write about ourselves
and rivers, he said, are erasers provided by nature.

She hands you a drawing of her soul.
Gold and purple skies, a lotus drifts across a lake,
dreams step softly behind closed doors.
She tells you the gypsy woman saw balance in her life
and as you try to think of your own soul,
Stalin rises from the wheat.
In every city of Europe blindfolded statues
hold up broken scales in their hands. You dream
one thousand faces burnt like the faces of your parents
on their Russian-refugee passports.

At night, your eyes roam for hours across your cracked ceiling
and as you think of the balance in your life
objects go tumbling down bottomless years
or float like drowned memories
on the waters forming half of the planet
that is really you.
At night, you remember Sunday school
and priests swearing everyone would burn in hell
and how at times you would watch your face
light up the bus station mirror.

Stalin rises from the wheat
and every homeless person you pass by,
every building weeping broken glass,
letters you never wrote, faces
drowned in rivers running through your poems,
every child shot, staring
from dark curtains of newspapers prints,
they all rise from wheat fields that stretch
from fire to fire and river to river
on the small planet that is really you.

Yes, Stalin rises from the wheat
and it's Sunday, the air filled with kites,
with ancient knowledge and you watch them go
like Russian émigrés rising over
the poverty of their messed up lives, like angels
sort of waiting for their inexorable downfall
and your father tells you he can feel
the elasticity of the sky through the kite
pulling on its rope, like a dog pulling on its leash
suddenly sensing happiness, one hundred yards away.

Your father tells you there's no direction
because gravity's gone.
The air is filled with kites
and ancient knowledge and you see hands
rising everywhere trying to grasp clouds,
emptiness running down fingers
like prayers at poorly attended churches,
like pages of your last read book.
You and Dick Stanley banging on the doors of life
and all of us on our planet, falling through the stars.

Stalin rising from the wheat
and gravity leaving our bodies
so we too can rise above
the poverty of our messed up lives.
This is a picture of my soul:
my parents, in this late hour
somewhere in Paris
in their small apartment
leaning over the lame dinner table
their faces burnt orange and

exiled between banks and chestnut trees
statues of defunct heroes look up,
their arms embracing empty spaces,
their eyes reflecting the absence of things.
They stand oblivious to the rain, to the snow,
oblivious to changing times.
Their faces register no emotion
at so much pain roaming our restless world
and all these kites, rising for a moment and
doomed forever to touch the wind and fall.

IV Tarnished Halo

The Best

Things are free, said the singer.
If you love sunsets you never
go to bed unhappy.

There's no sunset for graveyard workers,
only neon light dropping halos
on the dark linoleum floor.

No sunset for the starving
only a broken egg dripping
on the blue cloth of the sky.

No sunset for the unemployed
only a need not apply sign posted
by the smoke of factories closing down.

No sunset for the unlucky in love
only broken hearts floating away
into the red void of 9 pm.

No sunset for the depressed
only pools of blood
in recurrent dreams of

wounded clouds and white horses
stampeding East, always East.
No sunset for prisons

only stars and stripes floating,
stripes of snow
stripes of blood.

The best things are free and
green fields do not stretch for the poor
like $ bills they always wanted

to touch as they held
coins in their clenched fists.
Gold paved highways do not run

through dreams of petroleum unfolding
in the sleep of bankrupt oilmen,
and the best things do not come

easy in a poem singing
life long after
the sun has set.

Grief

This city wasn't different,
men and women moving
between blocks and years
chiseling them into chess pieces,
divine intervention dumping them
right into that street
where check-mate was
waiting to unfold.

This city stood
like any other city,
black windows, white curtains,
buses zigzagging
past fields of marigolds,
red houses, blue skies
and poetry flowing
past office glass.

Those who never dreamed
poetry, dreamed office buildings,
dreamed policemen, dreamed money,
copper coins rolling down their eyes
through alleys connecting
the dead ends of their lives,
all the way to a wilderness
some called the cosmic scheme of things.

Many waited for the harsh queen
to make its oblique move,
they were nothing more than pawns,
believing the losses of many
would add up to their big win,
never knowing they were grieving
poetry, unread stanzas a darkness
on the pale halos of their gods.

Urban Landscape

I memorized every brick in the slum
houses of Chicago, and Hispanic ghettos are
some of the forgotten pieces of my sleep.
I inhaled fear in New York

and watched many die where I lived.
Buses filled to capacity with workers
sinking below the line have left
their tire marks on my face.

Decay and ashes float on my lips.
Wind runs over my dark body.
For hours, I stare at the sun, waiting
for the sky to blink.

Days stumble, a procession of homeless
headed into night and nights all lie
down to die, growing
at dawn paler than stars.

Months come, years go.
Spoken languages slowly change.
I stare at the sky and sometimes the sky
blushes, guilt written all over it.

I am the street everyone said would turn bad,
the very street, running now whichever way
through the deep winter of every passerby mind.
Guilt lies unnoticed in that drifting snow.

Understanding The Homeless For One Moment

Look straight into his eyes, and
you'll see New York high rises,
Los Angeles one-way signs,

Houston overheated asphalt,
Chicago slaughterhouse skies, Detroit
dark windows and missing heart.

Catching the intensity of your stare,
like white light going through a prism,
he will divide into his many selves.

Part of him will hear far off
the drone of the great earth,
hear the great river flow

and for a moment, you too will grasp
the lisping of agitated trees
the liquid motion of clouds.

For a moment, you too will grasp
the homeless, his lips inhaling bitterness
his sky, paved with bad weeks

his memories, rusted knives across slippery years
his eyes, a dumping ground for broken windows.
You and he will drift

apart through winding alleys,
hot wind across your faces
like a lethal dream.

I Write About The Failures Of My Life

Buffalo Bayou runs past my home,
its Indian eyes unreadable and cold.
Rain wrinkles the surface of its face.
Oil spills put war paint on the tired features.
Today, I lean over muddy waters, hoping for
I don't know what.

Many times I've looked
at my own reflection
on twisted surfaces of metal,
on glasses filled with cheap beer,
on windows of passing trains,
trying to see myself through distortion.

Colors assemble, trying hard to paint
a picture of emigration:
white streets, blue houses, red sky
and surfacing from deep waters
here is my reflected face
with two stars for eyes.

I grew up Russian. I grew up French
and I grew up American,
always speaking a foreign language
wherever I lived.
People tried to guess where I was from;
you're Syrian, Italian, Greek, they would say.

My double blinks his stars.
He grabs a pen and scribbles
bilingual on the muddy bank,
his pen blazes like the unwritten pages of my draft.
Sur mon front, l'endroit sensible où le poème s'inscrit,
rain on my face sketches roads to new continents.

Wherever I go, I carry bankrupt landscapes.
In crowded bars, I like to play back
the failures of my life
and drinking coffee, I swallow night
and the two teaspoons of sugar I take
are ashes of poems I never wrote.

The windows of my room are prisms.
At night I lie awake, my body sweating colors.
Air presses against me like water and
I can hear the soft whisper of my lamp talking
to windows, walls and the lone door.
Its words leave dark stains on the ceiling.

You never amount to anything,
my teachers would say.
You will lose your hair by forty,
running with these women
my aunt always predicted.
My uncle didn't talk much.

At night, my lamp blushes pink,
the shade hangs crooked on its wooden frame
like hats worn by elegant women
who often look at clocks and
never understand how late it is.
The newspaper reads: Men desperately seeking women.

For a while I lived in my aunt's house,
came home late. I remember
the first woman I really knew.
Rose and her crooked hat with the wilted flower
and the twisted hotel stairs we climbed,
ascending to the 7th in a long question mark.

A drop of water runs down the lamp's shade.
I listen to my heartbeat and
the lamp goes on and off and on and off.
My shoes take on a rainbow hue
like the shoes in that famous picture
whose name I can't remember.

Rose, in her black stockings
standing by the leaking bidet.
Poverty naked on a red blanket,
mirrors on the ceiling shining
like some kind of benediction and
the sun dying behind closed curtains.

My shirt on the coat hanger
waves gently to the lamp
as if the empty cloth was leaving
the lamp with the crooked shade,
as if the room was a river
and I was drifting away from things.

Rose in her worn dress
no taller than a pencil,
waving a pink scarf and the train
picking up speed and I
feeling nothing, lean across years
watching Rose become a dot.

The high tide of night washes
other landscapes on the shores of my room.
Here's the city with one thousand towers
and angels with long twisted wings,
here's the sea, recording its music
on seashell phonographs.

After Rose, there was Beba
and then Janet and then Tanya
and then faces with no names
and then names with no faces
and then no names, no faces,
just years running wild.

Yesterday rain fell, Cyrillic letters twisting
Russian verses over deserted roads.
Today I write about the failures of my life.
A lazy sun stretches its golden arm,
draws three broken wings
on muddy waters flowing to no time.

Sometimes You Feel

Your body coming
apart and the world
is a photograph in hazy black
and uncertain gray. You look
at the future and
the future pushes forward
its armies of cloudy days waving
white flags of defeated hopes.

You try hard not to hear
the silence of your home.
Hours turn into days,
days into years.
The city sleeps. In its dream
you are a one winged angel.
A pale dawn rises over
the landscapes glued to your eyelids.

Scooping night with your wing
you jot down stanzas after stanzas
on the crumpled pages of your draft,
hard to read words spelling
the story of wounded angels,
bright flames flickering
then slowly fading
in the dark between the stars.

In The Subway

She feels her body coming
apart, like what was inside
wanted to run
away. She closes her eyes
and his face floats
in between trains.
His face now refusing
to fight gravity, slowly sinking
all the way down
to the rails.

His face a musical note
that can't be played
because her words ring foreign,
a heavy accent of Tundra
and broken gramophones.
The loudest sound is the train
coming and the rails humming,
dark and wet umbilical cords.
The train, shaking, screaming,
giving birth to separation.

Negative

When you close your eyes, nights turn
dazzling white on the tips of your eyelids
as if the stars had bitten off
pieces of their own hearts and were bleeding
light over the peaks, plateaus
and low points of your unruly rhymes.

Alarm clocks ring and hunger flows,
drowning every TV screen, the world
dissolving into salt and fog. Newspapers
headline the dead and the missing,
letters singing ancient
songs of bees mating in free fall.

You lift your hands to your face
and a distant star sets fire
to the names of the missing,
cinders coming down
from ceilings of concert halls, ashes
darkening the edge of music.

Snow swirls in a silver sky,
its whiteness invades your home.
Lamps blink, as if light
was trying not to light.
The way your shadow glides
is the reason mirrors,

denying optics, have started to reflect
no face, no light, no space,
no time. Mirrors showing
a world already faded.
Glass searching for that absence,
music crying over silent violins.

Revolutions Rise From The Page

This evening defunct railway stations erect
miles of rusted rails deep under my eyelids,
so I weep steam engines and cigar
ashes on the margins of this page.
October sits in public waiting rooms
trying to keep warm and remembers
how it lost the sun
way up over autumn mist
and northern guilt rises
thick as smoke of burning leaves.

October stares at evergreen trees
thinking them red just because
blood runs thicker than water. It boards
the train bound to deeper autumns and
wagons tumble like lizards losing
their footholds because walls come
crashing down when one winged angels
leave their stations, searching
for dishwashers to clean
their tarnished halos.

Don't you know blurred sycamores are
memories of runaway trains,
brothers and sisters to poems when they dodge
ink blots and bad images speeding on the page.
Sometimes the page is a snow field
however beware when the page
is simply a field of roses,
the pinkness of it may push
October to suicide, especially if it catches
elephants and burning bushes on T.V.

Revolutions rise from the page.
Letters escape raging fires
and take shelter in warehouses
where poetry books are jailed.
Poetry books unfairly blamed
by literary critics, purple because
IRS agents write odious poems
on unreported income pouring down
forty days and forty nights
over roofs of federal buildings.

Provincial newspapers curl up, their print
whispering the Latin patois of dead leaves,
headlines slowly fading because
paper mills never wanted politics to mar
the whiteness of the paper and
Sunday ads are the loss of salvation
for little publications trying hard
to live right from day to day,
now and then pulling tighter
their red rubber bands.

Little publications depressed
on account of rejected stories
such as one-winged angels falling
in love with sycamore trees and using
their lone wings as quills to write poems
and rails, sliding through angel poems,
imagine light on the other side of my eyelids.
Trains weep diamond lizards
right in between two stanzas on the page.
Two lizards, gentle smiles on burning walls.

Unwritten stories waving banners
which on closer inspection are no banners
but gaudy colors in the cheaply made
nightmares of librarians and this because
the chief librarian goes against the wind
which, all of a sudden, blows in blizzard ways.
He will not find salvation should he run
to the circulation desk screaming *Maman,*

because near the exit, a lewd foreign grammar
French kisses the milkman.

He will not find salvation because
chairs refuse to browse serious books.
Instead, they leave the library to watch
one winged angels moving
slowly through the park.
Palms give their hearts away
round and bruised like fallen oranges
and although misinformed policemen threaten
to arrest chairs for shady thoughts,
the wind sprays slogans on the sky.

Revolutions spread to rural landscapes,
invade streets where nothing ever happens.
Yellow clouds polka-dot the sky
and tuna fish cans expand and acquire
the threatening look of grenades,
ready to explode at a pin's drop,
filling up with desire for change
and dreams of lawyers sleep-walking
through foreign cities, lawyers all wanting
to snap the moon's silver threads.

Catastrophe sits on benches in small towns,
turning its multiple faces
towards banks, churches, schools
and the incredible tension building
on account of rain, ready to disrobe,
goes largely unnoticed because scarecrows
standing all day in hot wheat fields
have barely blinked
as gold and silver ripple
across their wooden faces.

The night wind spits sunflower seeds
over cities and small towns because
two bolts came unscrewed from my eyes
and the season of changes snakes
through impassable streets so that gas

lamps lean over, disapproval
written on their transparent faces,
their lights burning brighter than old beliefs,
when faces of generals and politicians sink
into the void of money wasted and wars lost.

Revolutions rise from the page because
moonbeams ascend faster
the old and creaking staircases
than they did back then, the same
staircases where absent minded lawyers
twist their ankles and judges
break their necks. Judges dying
and sand running down their eyes,
slowly seeping into courthouse clocks.
Deserts live in the unseeing eyes of judges.

One day sand will pile up higher than the TV tower.
Mirages will be born. Palms wave
torn calendars in their clenched fists.
It will rain hammers and sickles,
rain elephants, donkeys and the whole zoo.
Meanwhile roosters get ready
to crow their alarm from deep under
the robes of dead judges.
Angels grow second wings and the autumn wind
surprises me, blowing away steam

engines and ashes off this stanza.

At the end of the night
tuna fish cans sleeping
on the kitchen table are ready
to swim all over the vast floor
should a huge can opener
come down to stab them.
One more time my eraser
goes sliding through unstable worlds
and the stripes it leaves behind
begin to corrode everything

even the stars. Oh say
can't you see
what you so proudly hail'd
wasn't the twilight's last gleaming
only the rocket's red glare
o'er the land of the free
and the home of the brave.
Sliding through unstable worlds,
only defunct railway stations and
cigar ashes now left on the page.